YORKSHIRE'S LAST DAYS OF COLLIE

by

Tom Heavyside

Over the years many coke manufacturing plants were established at various colliery sites. From January 1963, under the National Coal Board, these were administered as a separate entity by the Coal Products Division. Here Hawthorn Leslie-built 0-6-0ST Works No. 3575, 'Coal Products No. 3', of 1923 vintage, is seen against the backdrop of Glasshoughton Coking Plant at Castleford on 21 August 1974.

Text and photographs © Tom Heavyside, 2005.
First published in the United Kingdom, 2005,
by Stenlake Publishing Ltd.
Telephone: 01290 551122
Printed by Cordfall Ltd., Glasgow, G21 2QA

ISBN 1 84033 330 8

ACKNOWLEDGEMENTS
I would like to express my gratitude to Paul Abell, Bob Darvill, John Fozard,
Chris Gee, Ivor Thomas, Don Townsley and the staff of Wigan Heritage
Service for their ready help in the completion of this volume.

Some collieries had to dispose of prodigious amounts of waste material, as at Peckfield Colliery, Micklefield, to the east of Leeds, where Hudswell Clarke 0-6-0T Works No. 1822 of 1949 (NCB No. S100) is seen attacking the fierce gradient towards the top of the tip, while propelling a set of side-tipping wagons, on 6 June 1972.

INTRODUCTION

There are two quite distinct regions to the coalfields in Yorkshire. The one in the south of the county was worked mainly in the areas around Barnsley, Sheffield and Doncaster, while the coal seams in the west were mined principally in the Leeds, Wakefield and Castleford areas.

As elsewhere, it was the development of the waterways during the eighteenth century, followed by the rapid expansion of the railway network during the Victorian era, which enabled the Yorkshire coal-owners to exploit their assets to the full. As regards the railways, it was in 1812 on the Middleton Colliery Railway, not far from the centre of Leeds, that steam locomotives were first used on a regular day-to-day basis, although the early locomotives utilised a 'toothed' rack-rail as an aid to propulsion, rather than relying on adhesion alone. Incidentally, the Middleton Railway was also the first to be sanctioned by an Act of Parliament in 1758, horses being the staple form of motive power in the early days.

As an indication of the subsequent development and importance of coal to the economy of Yorkshire, when the industry was vested in the National Coal Board on 1 January 1947 there were no less than 117 collieries spread across the county, with over 132,000 men employed in the extraction and processing of the mineral. Included among the assets taken over by the NCB were literally scores of steam locomotives. These were used for internal shunting at the pits and transferring vast tonnages of coal to the exchange sidings where it was collected by main line locomotives belonging to either the London Midland & Scottish Railway or the London & North Eastern Railway (both becoming part of British Railways from January 1948). In some locations the coal was carried to canal or river staithes for onward transmission.

Twenty-three years later, in January 1970, and almost eighteen months after the end of steam on British Railways, the NCB in Yorkshire owned no less than 112 steam locomotives. Eight of their number, administered by the Coal Products Division, were allocated between two coking plants and a by-products plant, with one, ex-LMS 'Jinty' 0-6-0T No. 47445, at the Opencast Executive British Oak Disposal Point at Crigglestone, near Wakefield. No. 47445 had been purchased from BR in May 1966. The remaining 103 were divided between the four NCB Yorkshire areas as follows – North Yorkshire (35), Doncaster (9), Barnsley (32) and South Yorkshire (27), with thirty-eight collieries having one or more on their books. However, it should be stated that much of the locomotive work, particularly in the Doncaster and South Yorkshire areas, had already been taken over by a fleet of ninety-nine diesels along with one engine that was powered by methane, with three electric locomotives being employed on

coke oven duties.

Eighty-two of the steam stud had originated in the factories of three Yorkshire-based private locomotive builders, fifty-one having been constructed by the Hunslet Engine Co. Ltd and twenty-six by Hudswell Clarke & Co. Ltd, both of Leeds, with the Yorkshire Engine Co. Ltd of Sheffield being responsible for the other five 'home-grown' products. The remaining thirty had been put together by seven other manufacturers. The most dominant type were the eighty-two 0-6-0s fitted with a saddle tank, aided by fifteen 0-6-0s which carried their water supplies in side tanks, along with thirteen 0-4-0STs and two 0-6-0 fireless engines. While seventy-six of the locomotives were less than thirty years old there were also a few veterans around, with six dating back to before the First World War, including two from 1900 – Hawthorn Leslie 0-4-0ST Works No. 2454 at Smithywood Coking Plant at Chapeltown, near Sheffield, and Peckett Class 'X' 0-6-0ST Works No. 836 at Cadeby Main Colliery at Conisbrough. The former was built in Newcastle-upon-Tyne and the latter in Bristol.

Listed amongst the stock in 1970 were thirty-eight of the Hunslet-designed 'Austerity' 0-6-0STs which had been introduced in 1943 to aid the war effort, with examples from all six wartime suppliers of the class to the Ministry of Supply being represented. Eight of the total had been built new for the NCB between 1948 and 1964, the two constructed during the latter year bringing the class total to 485. The other thirty had been purchased second-hand, the first five in 1946, just prior to Nationalisation, with the last not touching NCB metals until 1965. Previous owners included the Port of London Authority and British Railways (ex-'J94' class Nos. 68020, 68067 and 68077), as well as the army.

During the early 1970s, in addition to the 'Austerities', the NCB also made good use of some slightly less powerful engines, among them a batch of Hunslet 0-6-0STs with 15in. or 16in. diameter cylinders (the 'Austerities' had 18in. cylinders), some Hudswell Clarke 0-6-0Ts and a few 0-4-0STs from the same company. In the main, it was the engines built after 1940 that were most regularly fired, although one or two of the older machines could sometimes be seen in steam.

Visitors to the Yorkshire coalfields during the 1970s would have noticed the 'Austerity' 0-6-0STs had conical-shaped chimneys, and many of the other working locomotives stovepipe versions. These fitments indicated the engine concerned had been adapted (or in a few cases built new) with a Hunslet underfeed stoker and gas producer system that had been developed by the company during the early 1960s with the aim of reducing the incidence of black smoke, at a time when officialdom was becoming

increasingly concerned regarding the provisions of the 1956 Clean Air Act. However, in many instances, it quickly fell into disuse due to increased maintenance requirements compared to conventional firing and the oft-times unavailability of suitable small coals that the mechanical stoker was designed to feed into the firebox.

As the 1970s progressed the stock of steam locomotives was gradually reduced, and in January 1979 there were only eleven listed on the various inventories: six in the North Yorkshire Area, two in the Barnsley Area, with a further two at the coking plants and one 0-6-0 fireless locomotive at Manvers Main By-Products Plant at Wath-upon-Dearne, near Mexborough, attached to the Coal Products Division. By this time the Doncaster and South Yorkshire areas, as well as the Opencast Executive, had eradicated the iron horse from their respective territories. Despite their reduced numbers, isolated pockets of steam working lingered on into the early 1980s, before steam was dispensed with altogether and the diesels gained a total monopoly of the remaining locomotive work.

Today, there is still some mining activity within the White Rose county, although on a much reduced scale from the days when it was one of the main industries of the region. The few mines that remain are, of course, now back in private hands, but for those who desire a taste of the industry as it was in times past then a visit to the National Coal Mining Museum for England, based at the former Caphouse Colliery at Overton, between Huddersfield and Wakefield, is recommended. Part of the trackbed of the erstwhile Middleton Colliery Railway in Leeds is still in use as a heritage railway, while thirty-three of the former Yorkshire-based NCB steam locomotives that survived into the 1970s have been preserved. Eleven of these remain in Yorkshire, including seven at the Embsay & Bolton Abbey Railway, near Skipton, while the rest have been widely dispersed amongst various sites around the United Kingdom.

This volume looks back to the days when I enjoyed numerous day trips away from my Lancashire roots in order to record the last days of Yorkshire steam in industrial use, a time when steam locomotives still played a role in moving the black diamonds away from their source to wherever they were required to produce heat, light and energy. I always feel fortunate in having had the opportunity to witness some of these last hours, the final movements in the autumn of 1982 being the culmination of 170 years of vital work that had begun back in 1812 at the Middleton Colliery Railway in Leeds. They certainly were truly memorable days.

Being prepared for duty: the driver tops up one of the sandboxes of Hunslet 0-6-0ST Works No. 1956 of 1939 (NCB No. S111), 'Airedale No. 2', at Savile Colliery, Methley, on 28 March 1974.

Thirty-three of the engines domiciled in the Yorkshire coalfields at the start of 1970 have been saved for posterity: this is 'Beatrice', an 0-6-0ST built by Hunslet in 1945 (Works No. 2705) and previously of Ackton Hall Colliery, Featherstone (see page 27). She is hauling a train away from Embsay Station on the Embsay & Bolton Abbey Railway, near Skipton, an ex-Midland Railway line that once linked Skipton with Ilkley. On the right is sister 0-6-0ST, Works No. 3783 of 1953, 'Darfield No. 1', one-time of Darfield Main Colliery at Wombwell, near Barnsley. Like so many of the preserved engines, 'Darfield No. 1' has since moved away from the White Rose county and is now resident on the Llangollen Railway in North Wales. The picture was taken on 8 June 1986.

Preparatory work on sinking the shafts at Markham Main Colliery, Armthorpe, two miles east of Doncaster, began in 1914, but within a few months the operation had to be curtailed due to the outbreak of the First World War. It was May 1924 before any coal was hoisted to the surface, this being excavated from the famed Barnsley Seam. The colliery was connected to the South Yorkshire Joint Railway, which ran from Dinnington, in the south, to Kirk Sandall in the north. Only opened in January 1909, the main purpose of this undertaking by the Great Central, Great Northern, Lancashire & Yorkshire, Midland, and North Eastern railways, was to carry coal from the various mines established along its 17½-mile length during the early years of the twentieth century. Like the other pits situated close to the route, Markham was a large concern and, for instance, in 1947 produced 720,000 tons of coal and employed 2,470 men. The colliery was closed by British Coal, as the NCB was then known, in October 1992. It was subsequently reopened by Coal Investments Ltd in January 1995, only for it to be closed again in September of the following year.

The pictures on this and the previous page, taken on 29 March 1974 when the pit was administered by the NCB Doncaster Area, depict Hunslet-built 0-6-0ST Works No. 3782 of 1953 shunting wagons around the colliery yard. It was officially named 'Arthur', although there was no evidence of any nameplates at this time. During the early 1920s the Hunslet Engine Company developed a standard range of 0-6-0 locomotives suitable for industrial sites, 'Arthur' being one of forty-four built with 16in. x 22in. inside cylinders and 3ft 9in. diameter wheels between 1923 and 1958. The class was able to exert a nominal tractive effort of 17,022lb. at 85% of maximum boiler pressure (160lb. per square inch), although the Hunslet catalogue quoted 15,020lb. based on 75% of maximum boiler pressure. They were capable of hauling a load of 795 tons along level track, 390 tons up an incline of 1-in-100, and 225 tons up a gradient as steep as 1-in-50. A rigid wheelbase of 11ft 0in. allowed the engines to traverse with ease minimum radius curves of 180ft. Weight in full working order was 38 tons 15cwt. 'Arthur' was last used at Markham early in 1976. Pleasingly it is still extant, although now in more southern climes at the Buckinghamshire Railway Centre at Quainton Road, near Aylesbury.

When this photograph of Hunslet 0-6-0ST Works No. 3594 of 1950, 'Rossington No. 1', was taken outside the two-road shed at Askern Main Colliery, Askern, some six miles to the north of Doncaster, on 29 March 1974, its working days had already come to an end. The engine, built to the same specifications as 'Arthur' at Markham Main, had until June 1968 been based at Rossington Colliery, on the south side of Doncaster, hence its name. Later, in March 1977, when the rest of the locomotive was dismantled for scrap, the boiler was despatched to the Steamport Transport Museum at Southport, as a replacement for that on preserved sister locomotive Hunslet Works No. 1954 of 1939 (NCB No. 9), 'Kinsley', which had been recovered from South Kirkby Colliery (see page 18). Also on view is another Hunslet product (Works No. 5647 of 1960), ex-British Railways 0-6-0 diesel-mechanical shunter No. D2598. It was purchased by the NCB from BR in May 1968, and prior to arriving at Askern in July 1971, it too had worked at Rossington where it was given the name 'Sam'. No. D2598 was scrapped in May 1975. On the right are a couple of side-tipping 'Jubilee' wagons used for carrying colliery waste to the tip. The colliery itself, which in the early 1960s had employed over 1,800 men, was shut down in December 1991, after providing coal for nigh on eighty years.

Opposite: Cadeby Main Colliery at Conisbrough, near Mexborough, had the distinction of operating the very last steam locomotive built for normal everyday commercial use in Britain. The engine in question was yet another of the well-proven Hunslet 'Austerity' 0-6-0STs, which left their Jack Lane factory in Leeds without ceremony as Works No. 3890 (NCB No. 66) on 27 March 1964. Cadeby Main, along with its near neighbour on the opposite side of the River Don, Denaby Main Colliery, was owned by Denaby & Cadeby Main Collieries Ltd until March 1927, when the company was taken over by Yorkshire Amalgamated Collieries Ltd. During the first year of state ownership, 1947, Cadeby hoisted 525,000 tons of coal to the surface and Denaby 610,000 tons, with Cadeby employing 1,490 men and Denaby 1,970. During the 1950s the NCB invested over £4 million in the site, with the Denaby coal being wound at Cadeby from 1956 by way of an underground connection, although the two were not actually merged until May 1968, after which, officially, Denaby no longer existed. No. 66 had been idle for some time when photographed outside the shed in March 1974, diesels then having sole charge of the complex, one of which can just be seen in the doorway on the right. Note the conical-shaped chimney on No. 66, which it had carried from new, a distinguishing feature of the 'Austerities' fitted with the Hunslet underfeed stoker and gas producer system. Appropriately, the engine still survives, although now far away from its Yorkshire roots, at the Quainton Road home of the Buckinghamshire Railway Centre, near Aylesbury. As for the colliery itself, this closed in November 1986.

In former days, Smithywood (sometimes spelt Smithy Wood) Colliery at Chapeltown, four miles north of Sheffield city centre, was owned by Newton Chambers & Co. Ltd. During the 1920s the company decided to replace a number of its small coking plants in the area with a battery of fifty-nine W.D. Becker coke ovens constructed at Smithywood, so as to concentrate the production of this important fuel at this one outlet. Coal from the company's other pits in the district was transported by a series of aerial ropeways, that from Rockingham stretching for over four and a half miles, although latterly all coal was brought in by road. The colliery at Smithywood ceased production in December 1972, but the coking plant remained in use until 1986 when the ovens were finally extinguished. Following the removal of some coal by opencast methods, the site is now occupied by various industrial units.

From 1964 most of the locomotive duties were in the hands of a couple of Hunslet-built 'Austerity' 0-6-0STs. This robust class of engine with 18in. x 26in. cylinders, 4ft 3in. diameter wheels and a nominal tractive effort of 23,870lb., were highly suited to the conditions and type of work encountered at the coking plants and collieries. The photographs on these two pages include wasp-striped Works No. 3193, originally delivered to the Ministry of Supply in November 1944 as WD No. 75142. During its army career it served at a number of installations before being purchased back by the Hunslet Engine Company in 1962. Following a complete rebuild at their Leeds works, including the fitting of an underfeed stoker and gas producer system, and allocated a new works number, 3887, it was bought by the NCB and forwarded to Smithywood in March 1964 as 'SWCP No. 1'.

Left: 'SWCP No. 1' sojourns outside the rather dilapidated, corrugated tin-roofed, one-road shed on 24 June 1974.

Right: Later on the same day the engine stops briefly in the midst of shunting operations while the driver enjoys a short chat. Note the eight-plank wooden wagon on the right.

The pictures left and right depict 'SWCP No. 1' in front of the quencher at Smithywood Coking Plant, again on 24 June 1974. The engine had just dragged the car which carried the newly discharged red-hot burning coke the short distance from the ovens to the quencher, where it is being doused with water. Normally this duty was undertaken by a Greenwood & Batley of Leeds-built 0-4-0 electric locomotive, which drew its power from an overhead wire. Whenever the electric was unavailable for any reason then steam was called upon to deputise, as here. The plant could handle up to 440,000 tons of coal per annum and, as well as the production of coke, the by-products recovered included tar, sulphate of ammonia, rectified benzene and gas for town use.

The second 'Austerity' at Smithywood, 'SWCP No. 2', was in the shed when these photographs were taken. This locomotive, Hunslet Works No. 3192, had a very similar history to that of its slightly younger sister, having been despatched to the Ministry of Supply as WD No. 75141 in the same month, November 1944. When its army days were over, it too was purchased by Hunslet, rebuilt with an underfeed stoker, and then resold to the NCB, arriving at Smithywood as Hunslet Works No. 3888, along with 'SWCP No. 1', in March 1964.

Steam remained active at Smithywood until 1982. Happily, the two engines have both been preserved, 'SWCP No. 1' now being based on the Lavender Line at Isfield, East Sussex, while 'SWCP No. 2' is at Peak Rail near Matlock, Derbyshire. Today, both are painted as pseudo ex-BR Class J94s, Nos. 68012 and 68006 respectively.

During the First World War Newton Chambers & Co. Ltd established a service shaft at Skiers Spring, near Wentworth, to serve their Rockingham Colliery workings. In 1952, in order to extract the coal lying reasonably close to the surface, the NCB opened a drift mine on the site. Here, Hudswell Clarke 0-4-0ST Works No. 1891, 'HC No. 3', which arrived new in June 1961 and never worked anywhere else, transfers a couple of loaded wagons to the BR exchange sidings on 22 August 1972. On the right are the tracks of the former Midland Railway Sheffield to Barnsley line. A few years earlier the engine had enjoyed a brief moment of glory when it featured in the 1969 Ken Loach film *Kes*. The engine was broken up on site in May 1975 with rail traffic ending the following year. Rockingham Colliery was closed completely in 1979.

Dodworth Colliery, two miles west of Barnsley, had a rather chequered history. The first sods for the pit were cut in 1857 by J. & J. Charlesworth Ltd who, a few years later, disposed of it to the 1862-established Old Silkstone & Dodworth Coal & Iron Co. Ltd. In 1879 the mine had to be abandoned due to flooding, but twenty years on, in 1899, it was reopened by Old Silkstone Collieries Ltd. During the 1950s the NCB invested over £2 million in the colliery, including the provision of a new coal preparation plant. Total output in 1960 was 487,000 tons, with 1,052 men then being employed underground and 272 on the surface. On 11 May 1971 the first of the last batch of five steam locomotives built by Hudswell Clarke, 0-4-0ST Works No. 1889 of 1960, 'HC No. 1', shunts a few wagons at the colliery. The engine was reallocated to Dodworth from Monk Bretton Colliery, on the north-east side of Barnsley, in October 1968, when it joined its sister, Hudswell Clarke Works No. 1890, 'HC No. 2', which had been there since new in October 1960. 'HC No. 2' remained in use from time to time until early 1974 although, latterly, to maintain it in working order various parts had to be retrieved from its already out of service older sibling. Both engines suffered the indignity of being reduced to a heap of scrap metal at Dodworth during March 1975. Thus, regrettably, with the three engines constructed to the same design in 1961 suffering a similar fate, despite their comparative youth, none of the engines outshopped by Hudswell Clarke in the 1960s have been preserved.

A long-standing resident at Dodworth was Hunslet 'Austerity' 0-6-0ST Works No. 2857 of 1943. It arrived in April 1947 after service in Belgium as WD No. 75008. In 1965, during the course of an overhaul at their Leeds factory, the Hunslet Engine Company installed an underfeed stoker. Here, on 22 August 1972, the engine draws a string of loaded wagons away from the screens. Powerful floodlights atop the pylon on the right assisted the men working in this area after nightfall.

The 'Austerity' is seen here again, this time on 28 March 1974, transferring a short link of 'merry-go-round' wagons, filled with power station coal, to the BR exchange sidings (on the right-hand side of the picture), where BR Class 47 diesel–electric locomotive No. 47038 (later No. 47564) patiently awaits a full consist of wagons before departing. During the course of this manoeuvre, the NCB trains had to access the ex-Great Central Railway Penistone to Barnsley line, which effectively acted as a headshunt. On the left yet more wagons are being filled from the overhead hoppers.

Traffic is temporarily halted along the A628 Manchester to Barnsley road at Dodworth (even a police car was forced to stop!) while the 'Austerity' propels some 'merry-go-round' wagons towards the exchange sidings on 22 August 1972. These movements were controlled from the flat-roofed signal box, seen to the left of the crossing. In January 1976, after standing idle for nearly two years, the 'Austerity' was despatched to Cadley Hill Colliery at Castle Gresley, near Burton-upon-Trent, where it acquired the name 'Swiftsure'. Later, in February 1987, the engine travelled to its present home, the Bodmin & Wenford Railway in Cornwall. That same year, in June, coal production at Dodworth came to an end, although meanwhile the long-term future of the adjacent BR tracks had been secured. The line had in fact been 'freight only' since 5 January 1970 (Dodworth Station having closed earlier on 29 June 1959), but on 16 May 1983 passenger services were reinstated when the Huddersfield to Sheffield service was diverted this way so as to run via Barnsley, rather than following the more direct route from Penistone through Wadsley Bridge. Dodworth Station (to the right of the road) was reopened on 15 May 1989, and while the footbridge has been demolished, and the traditional level crossing gates replaced by automatic lifting barriers, the signal box still stands, albeit out of use and unmanned. The station is quite convenient for the Dodworth Business Park, which in recent years has been developed on the land formerly occupied by the colliery.

Yorkshire Engine Company 0-4-0ST Works No. 2474 of 1949, 'York No. 1', rests outside the engine shed, along with a couple of surface workers, at South Kirkby Colliery, some seven miles north-east of Barnsley, on 11 May 1971. The colliery, named after the local village, was founded by the South Ferryhill & Rosedale Iron Company of County Durham in 1876. However, they were unable to complete the development and the unfinished shafts were taken over by the South Kirkby Colliery Company in the early 1880s. Later, in 1905, the pit, along with Featherstone Main and Hemsworth collieries, became part of the assets of South Kirkby, Featherstone & Hemsworth Collieries Ltd. In 1930 the company sold some two million tons of coal and employed 5,850 men (2,260 at South Kirkby). During the 1960s, under the auspices of the NCB, by means of an underground tunnel, Hemsworth coal was also brought to the surface at South Kirkby, and at the start of the 1970s over 800,000 tons of coal was being despatched annually, mainly to Central Electricity Generating Board power stations. Almost all the coal was leaving in 'merry-go-round' wagons hauled by BR Class 47 diesels which utilised the connection to the former West Riding & Grimsby Joint Railway Doncaster to Wakefield Westgate line, a venture sponsored by the Great Northern and Great Central railways. At the turn of the decade into the 1970s there were five 0-6-0STs on the books at South Kirkby, two Peckett Class 'X2s', purchased from the Bristol-based company by South Kirkby, Featherstone & Hemsworth Collieries Ltd in 1914 and 1915, and three Hunslet-built engines, the oldest dating from 1923. However, the introduction of the 'merry-go-round' wagons had left very little internal work, and by the time of this photograph four of the aforementioned locomotives had already been earmarked for scrap. Some of their dismembered parts can be seen dumped near the shed to the right of 'York No. 1'. The survivor of the former quintet, Hunslet Works No. 1954 of 1939 (NCB No. 9), 'Kinsley', was last used here in the summer of 1974 before it departed for pastures new on the other side of the Pennines at Southport in Lancashire in November 1975. It is now at the Ribble Steam Railway in Preston.

Here, on the same day at South Kirkby, 'York No. 1' potters along towards the shed, to be seen on the extreme right-hand side of the picture with the large water tank in front. In tow are a couple of wooden-sided wagons which were used only within the confines of the colliery yard. In the background on the right are three sets of headgear above the shafts, two being partly enclosed. The deepest shaft reached 2,436ft below the surface. 'York No. 1' was a member of the Yorkshire Engine Company's standard 'Type 5' class, having 16in. x 22in. outside cylinders, 3ft 6in. diameter wheels, a wheelbase of 6ft 6in., and a boiler pressed to 180lb. per square inch, providing a nominal tractive effort of 20,516lb. When it left the manufacturer's Meadowhall Works in Sheffield in September 1949 it first went to Wombwell Main Colliery, between Barnsley and Mexborough. It spent all its NCB days in the Barnsley area, finally arriving at South Kirkby from Wharncliffe Woodmoor Nos. 4 & 5 Colliery at Carlton, on the north side of Barnsley, in February 1971. The engine left in September 1975, destined for preservation on the Yorkshire Dales Railway, near Skipton, now the Embsay & Bolton Abbey Railway. The colliery was closed in March 1988 with the buildings subsequently demolished. The site is now being developed as part of the South Kirkby Industrial Park.

North Gawber Colliery at Mapplewell, two miles north of Barnsley, dates from the early 1850s. In 1882 the pit was bought by Fountain & Burnley Ltd after the previous owners had stopped production due to financial problems. During 1947, under the direction of the NCB, 550,000 tons of coal were hoisted up the shafts for coking, gas and household use. That year there were 950 men on the payroll. Stabled near the engine shed on 28 March 1974 are, nearest the camera, Hudswell Clarke 0-6-0T Works No. 1857 (NCB No. N2), supplied to North Gawber in September 1952, and Hunslet 'Austerity' 0-6-0ST Works No. 3212, originally delivered to the Ministry of Supply Long Marston depot in Warwickshire as WD No. 71448 in May 1945. The latter was returned to Yorkshire in April 1964 following its acquisition by the NCB. As per the normal practice at North Gawber, the 'Austerity' is carrying a headlight to aid night-time working. The lamp bracket on No. N2 can be seen affixed to the top of the smokebox. Notice the wooden chocks under the wheels of the two locomotives and the eight-plank wagon No. NG144 sandwiched in between, as well as the old sleeper chained to the rails in front of No. N2 to prevent runaways. Behind the 'Austerity' is a rather battered T. Smith of Rodley (near Leeds) steam crane. Rising over the shed is part of the winding gear above one of the shafts, the screens being just off the picture to the right. The 'Austerity' was cut up on site during the spring of 1977, while fortune smiled more kindly on No. N2 which is now on the Swindon & Cricklade Railway in Wiltshire.

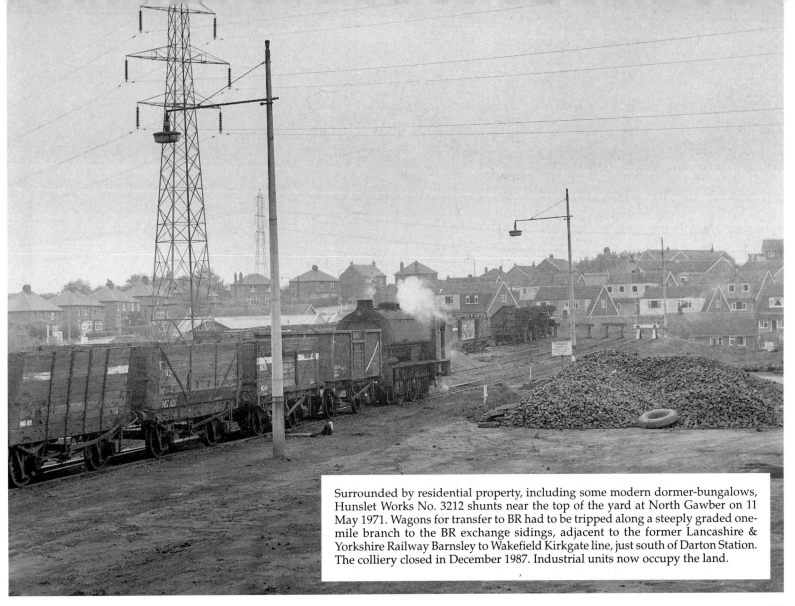

Surrounded by residential property, including some modern dormer-bungalows, Hunslet Works No. 3212 shunts near the top of the yard at North Gawber on 11 May 1971. Wagons for transfer to BR had to be tripped along a steeply graded one-mile branch to the BR exchange sidings, adjacent to the former Lancashire & Yorkshire Railway Barnsley to Wakefield Kirkgate line, just south of Darton Station. The colliery closed in December 1987. Industrial units now occupy the land.

The two photographs on this page illustrate the appalling conditions the NCB fitters had to endure at some locations. Here Hunslet 'Austerity' Works No. 3788 of 1953, 'NCB Monckton No. 1', is viewed through the broken shed windows at North Gawber on 28 March 1974. As indicated by its name, prior to its transfer here in November 1967, the engine had been allocated to New Monckton Colliery, South Hiendley, on the northeast side of Barnsley.

Inside the almost roofless shed on the same day 'NCB Monckton No. 1' was raised up on blocks while under repair. For company it had Andrew Barclay 0-6-0 diesel-hydraulic locomotive Works No. 553 of 1969, one time of nearby Woolley Colliery. The 'Austerity' re-entered traffic in June 1975 and an unusual duty later that year was to provide an anchor while a winding rope was changed. It was last steamed here at the end of 1977. It does, however, still remain in Yorkshire, although in a totally different environment, having exchanged the harsh realities of industrial Barnsley for the pastoral delights of the Dales around Skipton, on the Embsay & Bolton Abbey Railway.

When this picture was taken at Woolley Colliery, Darton, in March 1974, all that was left of Hunslet 'Austerity' Works No. 3208 of 1945 were the frames, wheels and bunker, the boiler having been retrieved in December 1972 for use as a spare at Cadley Hill Colliery, Castle Gresley, near Burton-upon-Trent. The engine was one of those purchased by the NCB from the army in 1965, and worked at Wharncliffe Woodmoor Nos. 4 & 5 Colliery at Carlton before it was moved to Woolley in February 1971. The remains were disposed of by Wakefield Metal Traders in June 1974. This left fellow ex-army 'Austerity' Hunslet Works No. 3183 of 1944, bought by the NCB in February 1963, as steam's sole representative at Woolley. It was last used during the winter of 1978/79 and is now part of the stock at Peak Rail, near Matlock, Derbyshire. As for the colliery, when the shafts were sunk during the period 1910–12, like its neighbour, North Gawber Colliery, just over a mile away, it was in the ownership of Fountain & Burnley Ltd. However, once steam had finished there was little life left in the pit, for despite the NCB investing over £100 million in the site during the early 1980s, including a new preparation plant to handle the coal from a number of outlets on the west side of Barnsley, the axe fell on the colliery in December 1987. The preparation plant did remain in use, but only for another four years until the end of 1991.

Coal from Emley Moor Colliery was washed and graded at screens located about one mile to the south by Skelmanthorpe Station, on the former Lancashire & Yorkshire Railway Clayton West branch. The coal was conveyed to the screens by means of an underground rope-worked narrow gauge line. During the early 1970s Hudswell Clarke 0-4-0ST Works No. 1817 of 1953, 'Standback No. 3', was held in reserve as cover for a 1938-built John Fowler diesel, and was observed outside the shed on 22 August 1972. The name 'Standback' was a reference to a former seam with a high calorific content, hence 'stand back!'. The engine shed was effectively two buildings built back to back, the difference in the brickwork marking the separate sections is readily apparent. 'Standback No. 3' remained on site until August 1976 when the men from Roe Brothers & Co. Ltd of Rotherham arrived with their oxyacetylene torch, a demolition job that was soon over. In the background, above the screens, can be seen the television transmitting station high on Emley Moor itself. The colliery wound its last coal in December 1985, although rail traffic had already been concluded in July 1982. Passenger services along the four-mile Clayton West branch, from its junction with the Huddersfield to Penistone line near Shepley, were withdrawn by BR on 24 January 1983. However, steam is again in evidence at Skelmanthorpe, as since 1991 the trackbed of the branch has been utilised by the 1ft 3in. gauge Kirklees Light Railway.

We commence our tour of the NCB North Yorkshire Area at Ackton Hall Colliery, Featherstone, a colliery with a history dating back to the late 1870s. It was a large pit and in 1930 produced 650,000 tons of coal, with 1,450 men working underground and another 400 on the surface. Facilities on site included a brickworks and fifty Simplex coking ovens. At the start of the 1970s output remained high with over 700,000 tons per annum being transported away. By that time both the brickworks and the coking plant had been closed down, although during the late 1960s a coal preparation plant was erected to replace the screens at the closed Snydale Colliery, situated one mile or so further west along the ex-Lancashire & Yorkshire Railway Wakefield to Goole line. Here, on 6 June 1972, Hunslet '50550' class 0-6-0ST Works No. 2414 of 1941 reverses towards the preparation plant. Design features of the '50550s' included a copper firebox, 18in. x 26in. inside cylinders and 4ft 0½in. diameter cast steel wheels. Eight of the class were manufactured during 1941 and 1942, five going to ironstone quarries in the Midlands and the remaining three, including No. 2414 to the War Department Long Marston depot in Warwickshire. However, from August 1943 No. 2414 was loaned to the Port of London Authority, before being added to their official stock list three years later as PLA No. 79. It returned north to Ackton Hall Colliery in October 1960, and was modified with an underfeed stoker in 1963. It was the only member of the class to be owned by the NCB. While at Ackton Hall it was numbered S112; the S prefix was a peculiarity of the numbering scheme adopted by the old NCB Yorkshire Division Area No. 8 (Castleford), the letter S being retained when it was handed down to the newly created North Yorkshire Area in March 1967.

Looking rather forlorn at Ackton Hall on 21 August 1974 are a couple of out-of-service 0-6-0STs. On the left is NCB No. 143, W.G. Bagnall-built 'Austerity' Works No. 2740 of 1944, rebuilt by the same company in 1954 as their Works No. 7079, and bought from the army by the NCB in 1965. It is in company with Hunslet Works No. 1440 of 1923 (NCB No. S106) which had been shorn of its 'Airedale' nameplates. The latter was one of the smaller Hunslet standard types with 3ft 7in. diameter wheels, a rigid wheelbase of 9ft 6in., and 15in. x 20in. inside cylinders. In all, twenty-seven similar machines were constructed between 1923 and 1947, 'Airedale' being the prototype and the first of thirteen destined for the Yorkshire coalfields.

These two photographs were taken at Ackton Hall on the same day as the previous photograph and depict Hunslet 0-6-0ST Works No. 2705 of 1945 (NCB No. S119), 'Beatrice', under repair in the workshop. 'Beatrice' was a standard Hunslet product with 16in. diameter inside cylinders – for other principal dimensions see page 7. The original chimney was replaced by this stovepipe version when the underfeed stoker was fitted in 1963. A distinguishing feature of both the 15in. (as opposite) and 16in. standard Hunslet designs was that the saddle tank did not extend over the smokebox. The chalked inscription 'Rovers' on the side of the smokebox refers to the local Rugby League side, Featherstone Rovers, which had appeared at Wembley only the previous May in the Challenge Cup Final when they lost to Warrington 24–9. They had had better fortune the previous year when they hoisted the trophy after defeating Bradford Northern 33–14. Three of the four locomotives seen at Ackton Hall, 'Airedale', 'Beatrice', and No. S112 (since named 'Spitfire'), were later to find a safe haven at what is now the Embsay & Bolton Abbey Railway, near Skipton, in North Yorkshire (see page 5 where 'Beatrice' is seen with a more usual style of chimney). Odd one out No. 143 was scrapped in July 1976. The NCB dispensed with the colliery in July 1985.

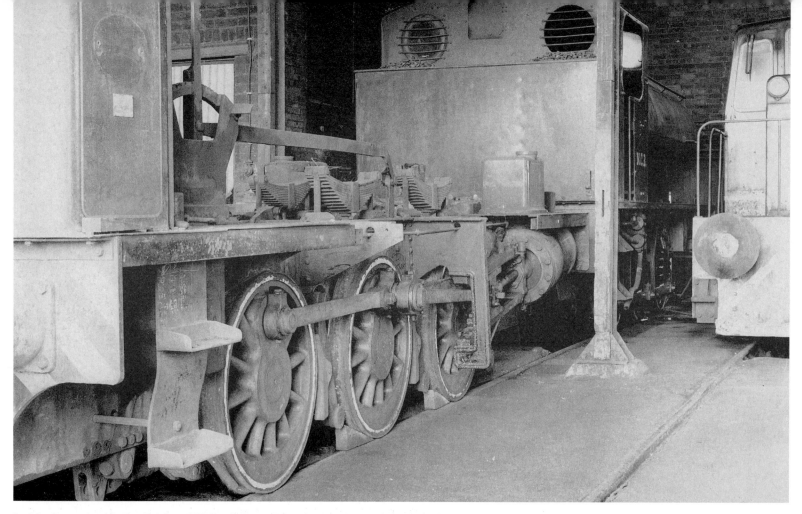

Inside the engine shed at Prince of Wales Colliery, Pontefract, on 21 August 1974, are the frame, bunker, wheels and motion of Hudswell Clarke 0-6-0T Works No. 1844, 'Whit No. 4'. It was put together in 1951 for Whitwood Colliery, on the west side of Castleford, and was transferred to Prince of Wales from Water Haigh Colliery, Woodlesford, between Castleford and Leeds, during May 1971. At the back of the shed is former WD 'Austerity' No. 75158, W.G. Bagnall-built 0-6-0ST Works No. 2746 of 1944, purchased by the NCB in 1965 and allocated number 144, while edging into the frame on the right is Hunslet 0-6-0 diesel-hydraulic locomotive Works No. 6685 of 1968. During the early 1970s over 600,000 tons of coal was being wound annually, mainly for sale to local power stations, the deepest of the three shafts reaching 2,145ft below ground.

On the same day at Prince of Wales Colliery the smokebox, boiler and firebox, together with the side tanks, belonging to 'Whit No. 4' were stored outside in the yard. 'Whit No. 4' was never reassembled and although the various parts were removed to the Nene Valley Railway, near Peterborough, in February 1976, they were used solely to provide spares for other engines. The Bagnall 'Austerity' was last steamed at Prince of Wales towards the end of that same year before leaving for Ackton Hall Colliery at Featherstone in January 1977. It was eventually preserved at Peak Rail, near Matlock, Derbyshire, where it now carries the name 'The Duke'. During the late 1970s the colliery was the beneficiary of a £74 million investment scheme, coal then being drawn from below ground by means of a new drift, with production increasing to over 1,400,000 tons per annum in the late 1980s. Later, following the privatisation of the coal industry, the mine became owned by R.J.B. Mining Ltd. The coal faces were finally abandoned in August 2002 after producing coal for almost 130 years.

Left: Prior to 1947, Glasshoughton Coking Plant at Castleford was owned by the Yorkshire Coking & Chemical Co. Ltd. Latterly, the plant was able to process up to 325,000 tons of coal per annum in forty-two W.D. Becker ovens, with tar, sulphate of ammonia, crude benzole, and purified gas for town use also being manufactured. With the plant in the background, Hunslet 'Austerity' 0-6-0ST Works No. 2897 of 1943, 'Coal Products No. 7', was looking somewhat down at heel as it awaited an appointment with the scrap merchant on a hazy 28 March 1974. This former WD locomotive (No. 75048) was acquired by the NCB in 1963, shortly after it had been rebuilt in Hunslet's workshops as Works No. 3886. It met its doom in November 1974 when it was dismantled by Thos W. Ward Ltd of Sheffield, a company responsible for the breaking of literally dozens of BR steam locomotives during the 1960s.

Right: With enthusiastic steam driver Colin Davies (who continues to handle steam locomotives on the Embsay & Bolton Abbey Railway) at the regulator, and with the shunter clinging to one of the cab side rails, Hawthorn Leslie 0-6-0ST Works No. 3575, 'Coal Products No. 3', makes a further contribution to the pungent atmosphere that pervaded the coking plant at Glasshoughton, while vigorously propelling a set of wagons on 21 August 1974. The engine was supplied to the Yorkshire Coking & Chemical Co. Ltd from the maker's Forth Bank Works in Newcastle-upon-Tyne in October 1923, and was fitted with 15in. x 22in. outside cylinders and 3ft 7in. diameter wheels. Notice the builder's oval identification plate on the side of the cab, the steps attached to the saddle tank to aid the task of watering the engine (800gals maximum), the wasp-striped buffer beam, and the headlamp in front of the chimney.

Here 'Coal Products No. 3' is seen in the sidings by the ex-Lancashire & Yorkshire Railway Methley Junction to Pontefract Monkhill line, again on 21 August 1974. Slowly running forward with a brake van in tow is BR Class 31 No. 31209. The gantry supported a pylon for an aerial ropeway which carried spoil from the coking plant to the tip, and also protected the main line from any stray material that might fall from a swinging bucket while in transit. A couple of buckets can be seen above 'Coal Products No. 3', the upturned one on the left is returning empty from the tip. Behind the gantry is Glasshoughton Colliery, formerly owned by Glass Houghton & Castleford Collieries Ltd. Glasshoughton was variously spelt as one word or two over the years, the NCB favouring the single variant. There was a direct rail connection between the colliery and the coking plant.

During the same shift 'Coal Products No. 3' guides a set of wagons round the sharp curve that led from the sidings by the main line to the coking plant. Above the engine can be glimpsed 'Coal Products No. 7' (see page 30), and to its right the cooling towers of Ferrybridge Power Station, the recipient of vast quantities of coal over the years from various Yorkshire collieries. Coke production ceased in 1978, and the next year, in March, 'Coal Products No. 3' returned to its native North East, to the Tanfield Railway at Marley Hill, near Gateshead. The adjacent pit closed in 1986 and since then the area has been redeveloped as a vast retail and leisure park. A new station, served by the Leeds, Castleford to Knottingley service, adjacent to the spot where the photographer was standing, is due to open in 2005.

In 1915 Hudswell Clarke produced an 0-6-0T for the Port of London Authority at their Railway Foundry works in Leeds, a design that was to be perpetuated by the company into the mid-1950s. The class had 16in. x 24in. outside cylinders, a total wheelbase of 10ft 0in., the axles carrying the 3ft 9in. diameter wheels being set equally apart. With a maximum boiler pressure of 160lb. per square inch, the engines were capable of exerting a nominal tractive effort of 18,568lb. In full working order they weighed 41 tons 17cwt. The NCB bought fourteen of the class, including nine for various Yorkshire collieries, the last in 1955. The only marked differences of those supplied latterly compared to the earlier locomotives were a more angular cab and bunker, and a curved edge along the top of the side tanks. Two examples bought new by the NCB are illustrated on these pages.

Left: Here, at St John's Colliery, Normanton, the penultimate member of the class, Works No. 1884 of 1955 (NCB No. S102), 'Cathryn', hauls eight wooden-sided wagons past the large coal preparation plant on 24 August 1972, during a period when steam could normally only be witnessed in action on a Thursday morning while a diesel locomotive was serviced. From new in April 1955 until February 1969 'Cathryn' was on the books of Newmarket Colliery, Stanley, an underfeed stoker and the accompanying stovepipe chimney, which did little to enhance its appearance, being fitted in 1964. It arrived at St John's in May 1971, after receiving attention in the NCB Allerton Bywater Central Workshops, a facility established in 1959 by the then North Eastern Division Area No. 8 (Castleford) for the repair and maintenance of locomotives and wagons, along with other engineering requirements. From the early 1950s St John's also processed any coal lifted at Park Hill Colliery, Wakefield, which required washing, this being transported to St John's along a one and a half mile NCB-built railway. Prior to 1947 both collieries had been owned by Locke & Co. (Newland) Ltd. Rail-borne coal departed from St John's via a connection with the former Midland Railway Leeds to Sheffield line, although up until 1949 coal had also been able to leave by way of the Aire & Calder Navigation. The coal-cutters were last used at St John's in June 1973, with the washery being retained until March 1980. As regards 'Cathryn', following a short period in storage at Park Hill, it joined the growing ranks of preserved locomotives in March 1977, and, after being based at a number of locations in the Sheffield area, is now at the Elsecar Steam Railway, near Barnsley.

Right: With the pit head winding wheels towering overhead, Works No. 1864 of 1952 (NCB No. S103) is seen at work at Newmarket (previously known as Newmarket Silkstone) Colliery, Stanley, three miles or so north-east of Wakefield, on 23 August 1973. Notice the builder's plate (not the original) attached to the sandbox, above the cylinder, while on 'Cathryn', in the opposite photograph, it is affixed to the side of the tank, near the cab entrance. From the adjacent winding house, on the left, the cages could be lowered almost 1,100ft below ground.

With the shunter walking ahead, No. S103 hauls some empty wagons at Newmarket on 23 August 1973. Above the rear wagons a diesel locomotive can be observed outside the engine shed. The colliery was sunk by J. & J. Charlesworth Ltd during the late 1830s, the company only relinquishing ownership when the NCB assumed control in 1947. In the past coal could leave by two distinct rail routes. One exit was along a branch of the former East & West Yorkshire Union Railways which linked up with their Lofthouse to Rothwell line, near Robin Hood, an enterprise in which Charlesworth's had had a substantial interest in its early years. These tracks were closed in December 1963, leaving only the connection on the south side of the colliery to the ex-Methley Joint (Great Northern, Lancashire & Yorkshire and North Eastern) Railway's Methley to Lofthouse line. Further, until about 1950, there was also a colliery-owned line from the pit to a staithe on the north bank of the River Calder. The mine produced coking, gas, household and steam coal, in total 321,000 tons being brought up the shafts in 1947 when 1,130 men were on the payroll.

On the same day black smoke pours from the chimney of No. S103 as it returns from the sidings on the south side of the colliery. Delivered new by Hudswell Clarke to Whitwood Colliery, Whitwood, in October 1952, the engine subsequently worked at Water Haigh Colliery, Oulton, West Riding Colliery, Altofts, and Glasshoughton Colliery, Castleford, before it arrived at Newmarket in April 1973. Normal steam working was concluded early in 1976, only for it to make a brief but welcome return in June 1978 – when Hunslet 'Austerity' 0-6-0ST Works No. 3168 of 1944 was temporarily brought out of store at Allerton Bywater Colliery, on the north side of Castleford, where it had been since 1973 following an overhaul in the nearby Area Central Workshops – to take part in a BBC film, *The Hill of Heaven*.

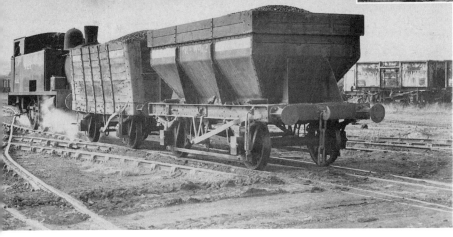

A few minutes earlier No. S103 had drifted by with a couple of well-loaded wagons. In April 1979 it was transported to Steamtown at Carnforth, Lancashire, but, after being incarcerated for twelve years from 1988 at Colwyn Bay Station in North Wales, has since become part of the stock of Dartmoor Rail, based at Meldon Quarry near Okehampton in Devon. Mining was concluded at Newmarket in September 1983.

Left: On 6 June 1972, standing outside the shed at Newmarket, is Hunslet Works No. 1726 of 1935, 'Jubilee', with a chalked instruction on the bunker, 'Light up for Sunday Morning'. The engine has a conventional-shaped chimney, being the only working 0-6-0ST in the NCB North Yorkshire Area not adapted with an underfeed stoker during the 1960s. On the left is the front-end of Hunslet 'Austerity' 0-6-0ST Works No. 2876 of 1943, 'Jess'. This engine had an interesting history. First, from December 1943, as WD No. 75027, it was loaned to the Ministry of Fuel & Power to assist at an opencast site near Ashington in Northumberland. Returned to the War Department in April 1944, it was then assigned to the Royal Victoria, Royal Albert and King George V dock complex (known collectively as the Royal Docks) on the north bank of the Thames. Along with other locomotives on loan from the WD, it officially became part of the Port of London Authority fleet in May 1946 as their No. 80. After being withdrawn by the PLA in 1959, it was sold to the NCB and despatched north to Prince of Wales Colliery at Pontefract in October 1960. The next month it was on the move again, this time to the Hunslet Engine Company Works in Leeds where, during the course of a full overhaul, it became the guinea pig for their newly-patented underfeed stoker and gas producer system. Emerging from Hunslet's in September 1961 with a rather ugly conical-shaped chimney, which hid the four-jet blast-pipe arrangement, it was transferred to Waterloo Main Colliery, on the eastern outskirts of Leeds, so that the equipment could be tested thoroughly on some lengthy NCB lines, and where it was also convenient for the Hunslet engineers to keep a close eye on its performance. It was while at Waterloo Main it was given the name 'Jess'. Incidentally, a miners' 'paddy' train had been operated at Waterloo Main until August 1959. The final move for 'Jess' was to Newmarket in November 1968, where it was scrapped in November 1973, 'Jubilee' having already suffered a similar fate in March of the same year.

Right: By the amount of dark smoke in evidence, the underfeed stoker arrangement was obviously inoperative on Hunslet 0-6-0ST Works No. 1956 of 1939 (NCB No. S111), 'Airedale No. 2', at Savile Colliery, Methley, on 28 March 1974. The engine had been allocated to the colliery since 1962. Both 'Jubilee', opposite, and 'Airedale No. 2' had 15in. x 20in. inside cylinders and 3ft 7in. diameter wheels. While they were not quite as powerful (tractive effort 14,232lb., maximum load on level track 664 tons) as the Hunslet 16in. cylindered engines (see page 7), they did have some advantages over their larger cousins in that with a shorter wheelbase of 9ft 6in. they could negotiate comfortably much tighter radius curves, down to a minimum of 120ft, and, with a total weight in working order of 33 tons 17cwt, were able to operate over slightly lighter rails, the minimum advised being 60lb. per yard as against 70lb. for engines built to the larger Hunslet profile.

'Airedale No. 2' drags an untidy bunch of well-worn wooden-sided internal user wagons towards the colliery buildings at Savile on 28 March 1974. Before the nationalisation of the industry in 1947, Savile was one of six collieries owned by Briggs Collieries Ltd of Normanton. In 1962 the colliery employed 332 men underground and 113 on the surface. That year they were responsible for the sale of 264,300 tons of coal. The pit was linked by a short branch to the ex-Midland Railway Leeds to Sheffield line, but this was little used after 1965, and in recent times most of the output was despatched from a basin on the Leeds branch of the Aire & Calder Navigation, mainly to Ferrybridge Power Station.

A couple of surface workers at Savile stop for a chat, perhaps debating the recent fortunes of Leeds United or one of the local Rugby League sides, as 'Airedale No. 2' drifts by on the same day.

Having returned to the shed, and with the shift almost over for another day, the driver throws out the fire of 'Airedale No. 2'. Despite its grubby appearance the lining on the paintwork is still very noticeable. The oval patch and the blank screw holes on the side of the cab, just above the alpha/numeric NCB number, indicate the position of the Hunslet works plate before it was removed. The engine was cut up for scrap in November 1975, while coal continued to be won from below ground until August 1985.

From the early 1950s, under the direction of the NCB, Peckfield Colliery at Micklefield, east of Leeds, also washed the coal raised at Ledston Luck Colliery, Kippax. In earlier days both collieries had been owned by the Micklefield Coal & Lime Co. Ltd, that is until 1937 when the assets were acquired by Briggs Collieries Ltd. Ledston Luck was shut down by Briggs in 1943, only to be reopened by the NCB in 1951, whereupon the coal was transported to Peckfield along a newly laid one and a half mile-long 2ft 6in. gauge railway. Diesel locomotives provided the power on the narrow gauge line. In 1962 Peckfield lifted 247,000 tons of coal and Ledston Luck 237,700 tons, with Peckfield paying the wages of 590 men and Ledston Luck 453. One of the main tasks for the locomotives at Peckfield was to propel 'Jubilee' wagons, sometimes referred to as 'dirt cans', laden with waste from the yard to the top of the tip. Photographed engaged in this work on 6 June 1972 were Hunslet 0-6-0ST Works No. 3715 of 1952 (NCB No. S121), 'Primrose No. 2', and, in the middle distance, Hudswell Clarke 0-6-0T Works No. 1822 of 1949 (NCB No. S100). Both engines had 3ft 9in. wheels and 16in. diameter cylinders, although No. S100 with a 2in. longer stroke (24in. as against the 22in. of 'Primrose No. 2') was theoretically slightly more powerful.

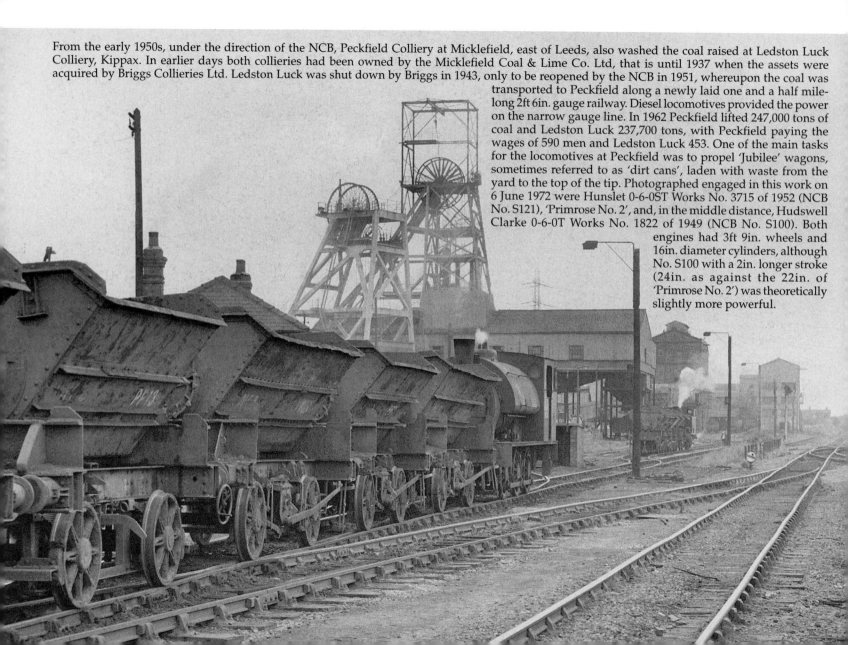

Later that afternoon No. S100 begins another assault on the vicious incline to the tipping site. The engine had resided at Peckfield since 1961. Behind the fence to the right of the wagons is the BR (ex-North Eastern Railway) line from Leeds to York and Hull, the junction where the two routes part company being half-a-mile to the east of the colliery, just beyond Micklefield Station. Peckfield signal box, which controlled the access points to the exchange sidings, is in the left background.

On 24 August 1972 at Peckfield, 'Primrose No. 2' bides time as the contents of a 'Jubilee' wagon are deposited on the tip, before it gingerly reversed back down the bank to the colliery yard. Prior to settling here in September 1971, the locomotive had previously only worked at Primrose Hill Colliery at Swillington, six miles to the south-east of Leeds city centre.

Here No. S100 blasts its way up the gradient towards the tip, as it pushes five 'Jubilee' wagons laden with yet more waste material from Peckfield on 6 June 1972. Steam working finished here at the end of 1972, although for a number of years No. S100 and 'Primrose No. 2' remained close companions, for in 1973 they both made the journey north to what was then the Yorkshire Dales Railway, near Skipton (now the Embsay & Bolton Abbey Railway). While 'Primrose No. 2' is still there, No. S100 was later transferred to the Chasewater Railway at Brownhills, Staffordshire. When Peckfield ceased winding in December 1980, the preparation plant was retained to wash the coal from Ledston Luck until October 1986, although from July 1982 the black diamonds were brought in by road following the abandonment of the 2ft 6in. gauge railway.

Wheldale Colliery at Castleford, sunk by the Wheldale Coal Company during the late 1860s, was on the north side of the former North Eastern Railway Castleford to York line. In 1919 the company became part of Airedale Collieries Ltd, a newly created combine. The colliery output in 1962 totalled almost 350,000 tons when there was a workforce of 792 men. Locomotive work included transporting coal to a basin on the south bank of the River Aire, where it was loaded into 40 ton capacity compartment boats known as 'Tom Puddings', these then being hauled by tugs in rakes of up to nineteen at a time to either Goole or Hull docks. In later years some 'Tom Puddings' made the much shorter journey to Ferrybridge Power Station. Any coal which required washing had to be taken along a circuitous one and a half mile colliery-owned line to the neighbouring pit at Fryston, and in addition there was a sizeable amount of dirt to be tripped to the tipping grounds on the opposite side of the river. On 6 June 1972 Hunslet 'Austerity' 0-6-0ST Works No. 2879 of 1943, formerly named 'Diana', approaches the level crossing over Wheldon Road as it returns to the colliery yard from Fryston. A diesel locomotive waits to follow with some empty wagons.

On the same day Hunslet Works No. 2879 delays an NCB-owned lorry as it propels a set of internal user wagons over Wheldon Road. The crossing was in regular use, a flagman being employed to ensure the safe passage of rail and road traffic alike. A further safety measure were a set of catch points on either side of the road. This ex-War Department locomotive had been a servant of the North Yorkshire coalfield since September 1946 when it was purchased by Briggs Collieries Ltd. It had been at Wheldale since June 1970, and stayed there until October 1973 when it left for Newmarket Colliery, Stanley. After being made redundant by the NCB it was moved to the Bowes Railway at Springwell, near Gateshead, in January 1975, before settling permanently north of the Border, on the Caledonian Railway at Brechin, between Dundee and Aberdeen, in July 1979. The last coal producing shifts at Wheldale descended the shafts in October 1987. A couple of winding wheels embedded on each side of Wheldon Road, and an avenue of trees planted as a memorial to those who lost their lives in the pit, or whilst serving in H.M. Forces, are a tangible reminder of a past era.

The colliery at Fryston, one mile east of Wheldale, was developed during the mid-1870s by the Fryston Coal Company. It was absorbed by the Wheldale Coal Company in 1899, and thus in 1919, along with Wheldale, became part of Airedale Collieries Ltd. In 1962, 538,000 tons of coal passed over the weighbridge, with 993 men working underground and 242 on the surface. The coal was used for coking, gas, household and industrial purposes, and could be despatched by road, rail or water, the latter by way of the River Aire. Here, on 6 June 1972, Hudswell Clarke 0-6-0T Works No. 1883 of 1955, 'Fryston No. 2', is about to pass 'Rose Louise', a 260hp diesel-mechanical locomotive put together by the same manufacturer, and originally supplied to Whitwood Colliery in 1956 as Works No. D972. The raised semaphore signal indicates to the driver of 'Fryston No. 2' that he can only proceed into the headshunt, alongside the BR Castleford to York line, past the engine shed – the south-east corner of the building can be seen on the extreme left-hand side of the picture.

A minute or so after the picture overleaf was taken, 'Fryston No. 2' was viewed near the end of the headshunt. The engine, another of the Hudswell Clarke standard 16in. x 24in. outside cylindered locomotives, was delivered new to Fryston in March 1955, and scrapped there in September 1972. Its only trip away during its relatively short existence was during the spring of 1964, when it visited the Hunslet Engine Company's factory in Leeds for the installation of an underfeed stoker. On the left is Fryston signal box and the associated semaphore signals which governed movements along the BR line (seen in the foreground), as well as entry and exit to and from the colliery sidings. Beyond the signal box, and behind the wagons on the right, can be glimpsed a few of the terraced houses built by the Fryston Coal Company to accommodate the miners, the somewhat isolated village, known as New Fryston, being hemmed in between the railway on the south side and the River Aire to the north. The only means of access to the village was via the bridge on the left. Today, only a few of the original terraces remain, the rest having been demolished along with the school and the Methodist Church after the colliery had been closed in December 1985. The colliery site has been grassed over.